The (Old) Isle of Dogs from A to Z
© Mick Lemmerman, 2014

Dedicated to Con Maloney and Peter Wright, fellow Islanders.

Akbar House Block of flats built on the West Ferry Estate in Cahir St., and opened in 1935. Like other flats on the estate, it was named after a Merchant Navy training ship.

Alastor House Block of flats built in the late 1960s on Strattondale St. and named after the sailing barque, Alastor, a frequent visitor to Millwall Docks.

Alfred St. Original name of Manilla St., changed in 1875.

Alexander House Block of flats on Tiller Rd. (formerly Glengall Road/Grove), built in the late 1920s, and named after Frederick William Alexander (1859-1937), Medical Officer of Health for Poplar and Bromley between 1893 and 1926. In 1931 he was awarded an OBE.

Alice Shepherd House Block of flats on Manchester Rd., completed in 1969, named after the chairwoman of the Housing Committee of Tower Hamlets Borough Council.

Alpha Grove Community Centre Alpha Rd. Methodist Chapel was built in 1887. An additional hall

Alpha Grove When built in the 1800s, Alpha Rd. followed a section of the old Island path, Dolphin Lane. Alpha Rd. was renamed Alpha Grove in 1939, and seriously damaged during WWII. The remaining houses in the rows of terraced houses were demolished to make way for 50s housing and, in the 1960s, the Barkantine Estate.

1. Alpha Rd.

was added in 1926. The buildings were converted into a community centre in the 1970s.

2. Alpha Grove Community Centre (Alpha Hall)

Anchor & Hope   Public house at 41 West Ferry Rd. Opened as a beer house in 1829, and closed in 2005. The building is still present.

Arethusa House   Block of flats built on the West Ferry Estate in Cahir St. Opened in 1936, it was the last-built of the 8 blocks on the estate which was built by London County Council. All flats on the estate are named after Merchant Navy training ships.

Argyle House   Block of flats built in the late 1960s on Marshfield St. and named after a merchant ship which was a frequent visitor to Millwall Docks.

Ash House   Along with other blocks on the estate, named after a tree sort in reference to the timber import in Millwall Docks.

Associated Lead   See *Locke, Lancaster & Co.*

Aste St.   Short street connecting the western ends of Roffey St. and Judkin St., in an area that was originally laid out by the Millwall Dock Company around 1900. Absorbed into Roffey St. when post-war housing was built in the area.

3. Anchor & Hope

Atworth St. Short street previously connecting Strattondale St. and Galbraith St., approximately at the location of the present-day Montfort House.

Barnfield An area of land purchased by the Ironmonger's Company in 1730. The company developed housing on their estate in the mid-1800s.

Barque St. One of three streets between Saunders Ness Rd. (then Wharf Rd.) and Manchester Rd. laid out c1860 and named with a sailing ship theme (the other two being Brig St. and Ship St).

Edward Le Bas Le Bas Tube Co. opened their first works on West Ferry Rd., before moving in 1898 to Cyclops Wharf. They were specialists in metal pipe and tube work.

Beecham's In 1945 Morton's was taken over by the Beecham Group, and the Morton's business was concentrated at Lowestoft, producing canned vegetables and fruit fillings. The Millwall works at the junction of West Ferry Rd. and Cuba St. were gradually run down.

John Bellamy & Son Bellamy's iron-tank works were set up in 1860 by John Bellamy, son of Edward Bellamy of the firm of Burney & Bellamy which had riverside premises nearby.

Betty May Gray House Betty May Gray died in 1933 leaving money *To Provide Or Assist In The Provision Of Housing And Associated Amenities For Persons Resident In The Area Of The Former County Of London And The London Borough Of Newham Who Are In Conditions Of Need, Hardship Or Distress, On Terms Appropriate To The Means Of Such Persons.* The Isle of Dogs Housing Society obtained £45,000 from this fund for the construction of what would be named Betty May Gray House (opened in 1962).

Billson St. Named for Jonathan Billson, builder, who was responsible for building the Builder's Arms pub and 26 houses in Stebondale St. (all destroyed in WWII).

4. Billson St.

Blacksmith's Arms   Public house at 25 West Ferry Rd. Opened as a beer house around 1895, and converted to a restaurant in 2001 (named Rogue Trader, but later renamed Aniseed).

Blackwall Basin   The entrance basin for the West India Docks, and built at the same time. Ships entered the basin via the Blackwall Entrance Lock (site of Preston's Rd. Swing Bridge) where they moored while waiting for a place to moor at a quay. Initially, the basin had no quays or wharves – these were mostly built from c1900 onwards.

Blue Bridge   Bridge over the West India South Dock eastern entrance lock. Opened in 1969, its design is based on traditional Dutch drawbridges. It is the 6th bridge at this location.

Bowsprit Point   One of the four tall blocks on the Barkantine estate, opened c1970. The four blocks, in combination with The Quarterdeck, are meant to represent a ship. The bowsprit of a sailing vessel is the pole (or spar) extending forward from the vessel's prow.

Bradfield St.   Short 19th century street west of the north end of East Ferry Rd. Later combined with Rushbrook St. to form Chipka St.

Brassey House   Block of flats built on the West Ferry Estate in Cahir St. Like other flats on the estate, it was named after a Merchant Navy training ship.

Bricklayer's Arms   Pub in short row of houses on the marsh wall close to Moiety Rd., first mentioned in the early 1800s.

Bridge House   Grand house built in 1819 just north of the Preston's Rd. swing bridge. Its first occupant was Captain Charles Compton Parish, the Dock Superintendent.

Bridge Rd.   The main road between Garford St. and the later City Arms (the section of road known as *The Walls*). Became part of West Ferry Rd. in 1937.

5. Blacksmith's Arms

Brig St. One of three streets between Saunders Ness Rd. (then Wharf Rd.) and Manchester Rd. laid out c1860 and named with a sailing ship theme (the other two being Barque St. and Ship St).

British Street School The first school on the Island, built in British St. (renamed Harbinger Rd. in 1930). The site was donated by the Countess of Glengall. The school premises closed in 1873, when the school moved to a new building across the road (the later Harbinger School). Badly damaged during WWII, the site of the original British St. School became a scrap yard.

Britannia Dock Dry dock built in 1863 by Rotherhithe shipbuilder and ship-owner, William Walker. It closed in 1935 and the filled-in site became a timber-yard, known as Britannia Wharf. The present-day Britannia Rd. is close to the site.

Broadway Works The name, Broadway Works, was first used in 1890 for a site leased from the Millwall Dock Company by George Clark, who had been a grocer in Westminster Broadway with a business manufacturing brewing sugar. The site was later occupied by Tate & Lyle Sugars.

Brown, Lenox & Co Manufacturers of ships' chain cable and anchors, mooring cables, mooring anchors and buoys, established in 1812. The Millwall works became part of the F. H. Lloyd Group and closed in the 1980s.

Builders Arms Public House at 99 Stebondale St. Opened in 1864, and destroyed in WWII.

Bullivant & Co. Established in 1914: wire rope manufacturers specializing in flexible steel wire hawsers and ropes, mining and hauling ropes, blocks, pulleys and all appliances for working wire ropes. It was one of eight companies merged into British Ropes Ltd on its formation in 1924.

Bullivant's Wharf Wharf belonging to Bullivant & Co, close to the original St. Luke's School on West Ferry Rd. Tragedy occurred on 19th March 1941 when an air raid shelter on the wharf received a direct hit during bombing. More than 40 people were killed and 60 injured. The event is commemorated by a plaque on Thames Path.

Burdell Engineering Engineering firm that operated on Ferry St. from the early 1950s.

6. Brig St., with Manchester Rd. in the background

7. Builder's Arms

Burrell's Burrell & Company, oil refiners and manufacturers of paints, varnishes and colours, established the Island arm of their business in the 1880s. The company was wound up in 1981, by which time it was a subsidiary of Ciba-Geigy.

Byng St. Named after George Byng (1764-1847), MP and member of the wealthy Byng family of Wrotham. His formal name was Viscount Torrington.

8. Cahir St.

Cahir St. Cahir St. did not exist before 1830, when a few small cottages were built on land leased from

William Mellish, and it was c1850 before the street appeared on any maps. Viscount Cahir was another name for the peerage, Earl of Glengall in Ireland (Mellish's daughter married an Earl of Glengall).

Calder's Wharf Named after wharfingers J. Calder & Company, who leased the site of North Greenwich Station when it closed in c1928. In 1969, a new boathouse for the Poplar, Blackwall & District Rowing Club was built on some of the site. The rest of the site is now used by a community centre, with new flats planned for construction in the area closest to Island Gardens.

Canal Dockyard An early 19th century (dry) dockyard immediately south of the point where the City Canal met the river in the east of the Island. The Pierhead Lock apartment development is now on the site.

Canal Row Original name of the section of Manchester Rd. now occupied by Glen Terrace. Named after former City Canal. Name changed in 1875.

Canary Wharf The northernmost of the West India Docks was the Import Dock. It was one of the largest docks, but its curved walls (i.e. curved below the water surface) prevented ships with deep draughts from mooring alongside. With increasing ship sizes, this was a problem as early as the late 1900s. The dock company's solution was to build 'false' quays, which extended out from the stone quay sides. These false quays had to be continually enlarged to keep up with ship sizes and, in 1937, a 580ft-long false quay was built on the Import Dock's south quay. It was named Canary Wharf.

The wharf was given this name at the request of Fruit Lines Ltd, subsidiary of the Norwegian Fred. Olsen & Co, because it was leased by them for the unloading of their ships bringing fruit from the Canary Islands. (An interesting coincidence – well-known but worth repeating – is that the Canary Islands are named from the Latin Islas Canarias, which in English is Islands of the Dogs.)

Capstan Square   1970s private housing development (the first of its kind on the Island) off Stewart St.

Cardale St.   Short street between East Ferry Rd. and Plevna St., created in the 1950s as part of the Castalia Square housing development.

Carvel House   Block of flats on the Schooner Estate, built in the early 1960s. Unlike other blocks on the estate, which are named after types of sailing ship, Carvel House is named after a technique for building wooden hulls.

Castleton House   Block of flats in Pier St., built in 1962 as part of the Manchester Estate. Like other blocks in the estate, named after an area of Greater Manchester.

Castalia Square   1950s development on the site of the former Castalia St. and Roserton St.

Cedar House   Along with other blocks on the estate, named after a tree sort in reference to the timber import in Millwall Docks.

Central Granary   A massive storage granary built on the west quay of the Millwall Inner Dock in 1903. It remained in use until 1969, and was demolished a year later.

9. Canary Wharf c1982

10. Castalia Square in the 1970s

Chapel House Place   Original name of Julian Place.

Chapel House St.   Named after the medieval St. Mary Chapel and Chapel House Farm. The chapel was first mentioned in 1380, but most likely was based on a chapel more than a century older than that. Remnants of the chapel were still present at the construction of the Millwall Docks in the 1860s, at the southern end of Millwall Dry Dock.

Charles St.   Original name of Malabar St., changed in 1891.

Cheval(l) St.   Richard Chevall was a London citizen and draper in the late 1600s. Chevall owned a 20 acre estate in Millwall. His daughter later married Thomas Tooke.

Chipka St.   Originally, the north end of East Ferry Rd. had two short side streets on the west side, named Bradfield St. and Rushbrook St. These streets were later combined to form Chipka St.

Christ Church (Church of Christ and St. John)
Christ Church was built by William Cubitt on land leased from the Countess of Glengall. The building was completed in 1855, and consecrated in 1857. In 1965, the congregation of St. John's church was combined with that of Christ Church, which was rededicated as the Christ of Church and St. John).

Church St.   Former name of Newcastle St., changed in 1891. Renamed Glengarnock Ave in 1937.

City Canal   A ship canal built by the City of London Corporation across the Island between 1800 and 1805. The canal was not a success, but later formed the basis of the West India South Dock.

City Arms   Public house at 1 West Ferry Rd. The original City Arms opened in approximately 1811, by the owner of the former Gut House. The pub was rebuilt in 1936, closed at the start of 2012, and was demolished in October of the same year. The City Arms was renamed City Pride in the 1980's.

11. Cheval St.

Clara Grant House   Block of flats opened (along with Gilbertson House) in 1952 on Mellish St. Clara Ellen Grant OBE (1867 – 1949) was a pioneering primary school teacher and later head at the Infant's School in Devon's Rd. around 1900.

Claude St.   One of three streets laid out close to Winkley's Wharf in 1857 by surgeon, Robert Webb of East India Dock Rd. (the other streets were Crews St. and Gaverick St). Significantly damaged during WWII, all houses in the street were demolished in the 1960s. After a period of industrial usage, new housing has been developed in the street.

Clipper House   Block of flats on the Schooner Estate, built in the early 1960s, named after a type of sailing ship.

Cold Harbour   The place name, Cold Harbour, is not uncommon in Southern England (more than 150 at the last count). The origin of the name is not certain, but most commonly accepted is that it is derived from the Saxon for a bare (or 'cold') shelter. The settlement of Cold Harbour was originally not more than a few houses on each side of a Thames embankment path.

College View   Small section of Saunders Ness Rd. The name was changed in 1937

The earliest known houses were built in the early 1600s. Known as 'Cold Harbour' for centuries, the spelling on street signs was changed to 'Coldharbour' for no apparent reason in the late 1950s.

12. Cold Harbour

Commons St. Short street between Havannah St. and Strafford St., disappeared on the creation of the Barkantine Estate.

Conway House Block of flats opened in 1933, and named after a Merchant Navy training ship.

Cord Way Short street formerly off Tiller Rd., a few yards west of the junction with Alpha Grove. Named after the Universal (Rope and Cable) Works that used to run along the entire north side of Tiller Rd. (then Glengall Rd.).

Cressall House Block of flats opened in 1951 on Tiller Rd. Named after former Poplar Borough Councillor and Secretary of South Poplar Labour Party, George J. Cressall.

Crews St. One of three streets laid out close to Winkley's Wharf in 1857 by surgeon, Robert Webb of East India Dock Rd. (the other streets were Claude St. and Gaverick St). Significantly damaged during WWII, all houses in the street were demolished in the 1960s.

After a period of industrial usage, new housing has been developed in the street.

13. Crews St.

14. Cuba St., 1997

Cuba St.   Name changed from Robert St. (after Robert Batson) in 1875. As with other streets in the area, it was named after places in the West Indies (a major source of sugar imports into the West India Docks).

Cubitt Arms   Public house at 262 Manchester Rd. Opened in 1864 and closed in 2011. The pub was built by Henry Smallman, also responsible for building The Queen. The building exterior is far plainer than originally, with the more ornate features removed in the 1960s.

Cubitt House   Block of flats built off East Ferry Rd. (close to, and at the same time as Roffey House) and demolished in 1988.

Cubitt Town   Named after Norfolk building contractor and politician, William Cubitt (1791-1863). Cubitt was Lord Mayor of London from 1860-1862. As well as extensive development in the east of the Isle of Dogs, W. Cubitt and Co. was one of the best known of London contractors, responsible for many important buildings, including Covent Garden, Fishmongers' Hall and the original Euston Railway Station buildings.

Cubitt Town Pier   Built by William Cubitt in 1857 at the end of Pier St. (which used to run as far as the river), and demolished in 1892.

Cubitt Town Primitive Methodist Chapel
Known locally as the 'prims', and sometimes referred to as Jubilee Chapel, this chapel was built on Manchester Rd., close to Glengall Rd., in 1869. It was completely rebuilt in 1904, and demolished in 1978.

Cubitt Town School   Originally, Cubitt Town School was located on Saunders Ness Rd. The first building opened in 1891, and in 1938 a much-larger replacement building was completed. This building was seriously damaged during WWII, and it was 1952 before repairs were completed. In 1970 the school moved to the former Glengall Rd. School building, and its Saunders Ness Rd. premises were taken over by St. Luke's Primary School.

Cubitt Town Wesleyan Chapel   Built on Stebondale St. (north side, close to junction with Pier St) in 1877. It was badly damaged during WWII and demolished shortly afterwards.

Cubitt Town Wharf The only original Island riverside warehouse still standing, now converted into flats. Built in the 1860s, it was first used for the processing and storage of rice, seeds and seed oil. Later uses included chemical works and rubber storage.

Cumberland Oil Mills Cumberland Oil Mills, next to the Newcastle Draw Dock on Saunders Ness Rd., were established in 1857, and were the scene of a floor collapse shortly afterwards which killed four workers. The works closed in 1964, and part was occupied by a scrap yard. The main warehouse was demolished following a fire in 1972. The remaining buildings were cleared away in the late 1980s for the Cumberland Mills residential development.

St. Cuthbert's Church Built in 1897 on the corner of West Ferry Rd. and Cahir St., on a site now occupied by Harbinger School playground. The church was destroyed by bombing in September 1940.

Samuel Cutler Samuel Cutler & Sons set up the Providence Iron Works in 1873 on the site of the former Millwall gasworks. They specialized in gasholders and other plant for the gas industry. The works (on both sides of West Ferry Rd., near St. Edmund's) closed in the 1960s.

15. Samuel Cutler Advertisement

Cyclops Wharf Cyclops Wharf was situated between the former Winkley's Wharf and Victoria Wharf. Previously, Powis Rd. ran here from West Ferry Rd. to Millwall Pier on the river.

From 1965 Cyclops Wharf was occupied by an asphalting and haulage concern, which in 1987 moved to Rainham. The late 19th century buildings survived until this time.

Davis St. Named after local builder, Charles Davis, who built 181 houses and shops and three pubs (Pier Tavern, Manchester Arms and London Tavern) in Cubitt Town around 1860.

Deptford Ferry Rd. Deptford Ferry was set up by the Poplar and Greenwich Ferry Roads Company in the 1800s. The road to its departure point ran from West Ferry Rd., at the location of the later Vulcan pub.

16. Deptford Ferry Rd. Sign on Vulcan side wall

Dock House Pub at 26 Cuba St. (corner of Alpha Rd.). Opened as a beer house c1850, and demolished in 1937 when this road junction was annexed by Millwall Docks.

17. Dock House

Dockland Settlement The Dockland Settlement organization was founded by Sir Reginald Kennedy-Cox and became a *haven of friendship, warmth and refuge from the squalid poverty outside*. The Island Dockland Settlement was the second to be opened, in 1923 in premises acquired from the Welcome Institute on East Ferry Rd. Much of those premises has since been demolished, and the whole has become a college.

Dolphin Lane A medieval lane that ran from Poplar (where a short road still has the name) down the eastern half of the Isle of Dogs to the current-day Tiller Rd. A short section of Alpha Grove follows it route.

Dorset Arms Four houses were built between 1860 and 1864 in a row known as Dorset Terrace. The builder obtained a license to sell ale and beer at no. 377, later extended to include no. 379. By this time it was already known as the Dorset Arms. In 1913, the two houses were demolished, replaced by the pub that was present until its closure in 1997 and subsequent demolition.

McDougall's In 1869, the McDougall Brothers (Alexander, Isaac, James Thomas, John and Arthur) opened their Wheatsheaf Mill in Millwall Docks, intending to exploit the market for their new self-raising flour. In 1934, the company built their iconic quayside silo (demolished in 1982).

18. McDougall's with Hawkins & Tipson's rope walk in the foreground

John McDougall's Park   Named after local mill owner and LCC councillor, Sir John McDougall. Built on the site of former factories and wharves, and opened in 1968.

Douglas Place   In the late 1800s – before the existence of Millwall Park - there were plans to build a road from the site of the current Island Gardens DLR station to meet an extended Newcastle St. (later Glengarnock Ave). Only a very short section was built, named Douglas St. In 1939 it was renamed Douglas Place.

Drunken Dock   A former dock, first mentioned in the 16th century, based on a natural tidal river basin. In the 19th century a mast house was built on its edge, using the basin for floating masts and spars. When sailing ships became obsolete, the mast house was closed and the basin was filled in. Mast House Terrace was built on the site.

Alexander Duckham and Co.   Based at his offices in the city, Alexander Duckham opened his Phoenix Wharf oil company in Millwall in 1914. Alexander was the son of Millwall Dock's chief dock engineer, Frederic Eliot Duckham.

Dudgeon's Wharf   John Dudgeon (1816-1881) and William Dudgeon (1818-1875) were blacksmiths from Scotland who founded an engineering shop at Millwall in 1859. A couple of years later they started shipbuilding in a yard directly south of Pier St. (which at the time crossed Manchester Rd. and extended to the river). It was the site of a major fire and oil tank explosion in 1969 which killed 6 men, including 5 firemen.

Dunbar House   A group of three blocks of flats opened in Tiller Rd. (then named Glengall Rd.) in 1932 and demolished in 1976. Primarily named after Dunbar's Cooperage that had been on the site since 1911 (owned by Canadian barrister and manufacturer, Alexander Dunbar), but with a nod to Scottish ship owner, Duncan Dunbar, whose highly successful shipping line operated out of the docks.

19. Dunbar House before and during demolition

20. East Ferry Rd. Dairy

East Ferry Rd.   The toll road from the eastern entrance of West India South Dock to the ferry at the south of the Island. Much of East Ferry Rd. followed the medieval Arrow Lane (later named Blackwall Rd.) from Poplar via Chapel House to the ferry at south of the Island.

St. Edmund's Chapel   Small Roman Catholic chapel close to Moiety Rd. which opened in 1846. It was in ruins by 1880, and was replaced by St. Edmund's Church.

St. Edmund's Church   Opened in 1874 on West Ferry Rd., and named after St. Edmund's Chapel. Demolished in the 1990s, a new church was built on the site.

St. Edmund's School   The original school was built at the same time as the church, in 1874. The school was replaced in 1909 and significantly extended in 1929.

Elm House   Along with other blocks on the estate, named after a tree sort in reference to the timber import in Millwall Docks.

Escott's Court   A small row of cottages off Cuba St. built in 1840 by William Escott, a local waterman and publican (he was landlord of the original Waterman's Arms at 6 West Ferry Rd.).

Exmouth House   Block of flats built on the West Ferry Estate in Cahir St., and opened in 1935. Like other flats on the estate, it was named after a Merchant Navy training ship.

Factory Place   A short road off Ferry St., now the entrance to St. David's Square. One of its earliest uses was as a herring smoke house, followed by a variety of different industries before its closure in the 1970s.

Farm Rd.   Traditional, informal name (still in use by some Islanders) for East Ferry Rd., almost certainly derived from Chapel House Farm which was on the medieval north-south road that pre-dates East Ferry Rd.

Farnworth House   Block of flats in Manchester Rd., built in 1962 as part of the Manchester Estate. Like other blocks in the estate, named after an area of Greater Manchester.

Ferry House   Pub in Ferry St. In 1700, the ferry to Greenwich departed from an area which was not much more than farmland. There was a starch factory near the ferry landing, and when this closed around 1740, the premises were rebuilt to become the Ferry House – probably serving refreshments to ferry passengers. The present Ferry House was built in 1822, making it certainly the oldest (still existing) pub on the Island, and one of the oldest buildings.

21 Ferry House

Ferry St.   Named after the former Greenwich Ferry, which was probably already in existence in the 1400s. Originally, Ferry St. referred only to the short section from East Ferry Rd. to the river.

Finwhale House   Block of flats built in the mid-1960s and named after the submarine HMS Finwhale, a visitor to the docks shortly before its opening.

Fishing Smack   Pub at 9 Cold Harbour. A pub was present at this location in the 1750s, then known as the Fisherman's Arms. It was rebuilt in 1893, and then demolished in 1948.

Folly House Tavern   Pub opened in 1758 in Thomas Davers' folly, and closed in 1875. The building was incorporated into Yarrow's shipbuilding yard.

Folly Wall   Formerly a path close to the river near Folly House. Later shipbuilding yards on the site belonging to Yarrow and, later, Samuda, were frequently referred to as the Folly Wall Yard.

Galbraith St.   Laid out in the 1880s, Galbraith St. originally ran from Glengall Grove to the corner of Roserton St. and Manchester Rd. Along with the rest of the area it was significantly damaged during WWII and was subsequently lined with prefabs. The street was shortened by the creation of St. John's Recreation Ground in 1966.

Galleon House   The tallest of the blocks of flats on the Schooner Estate, built in the early 1960s, named after a type of sailing ship.

Gaverick St.   Renamed from Gaveric St. in 1911. One of three streets laid out close to Winkley's Wharf in 1857 by surgeon, Robert Webb of East India Dock Rd. (the other streets were Crews St. and Claude St). Significantly damaged during WWII, all houses in the street were demolished in the 1960s. Gaverick Mews is now on the site.

22. Galleon House construction c1962. The rear of the police station is to the right.

George Pub opened in 1865, rebuilt in 1932, and still doing business. The original building was erected in 1864–5 by George Read, who was also responsible for 57 houses in Glengall Grove.

23. Jayne Mansfield in the George

George Green's School Founded by Poplar shipbuilder and philanthropist, George Green, the first school opened in East India Dock Rd. (corner of Chrisp St) in 1828, replaced in 1884 by a building also on East India Dock Rd. (corner of Kerby St). In 1976 the school moved to its current premises on Manchester Rd.

George St. Original name of Tobago St., changed in 1876.

Gilbertson House Block of flats opened (along with Clara Grant House) in 1952 on Mellish St. John F. Gilbertson was a long-serving member of Poplar Borough Council.

Glass Bridge When the dock company stated at the end of the 1950s its intention to close the Glengall Rd. bridge over Millwall Docks, protests and support from the council lead to the construction of a high-level footbridge across the docks, very quickly referred to as the Glass Bridge due to its glass enclosure.

The bridge became a target for vandals and pedestrians were so intimidated that few used it. Severe damage to the glass and the lifts in 1975–6 caused the bridge to be closed and it was demolished by the London Docklands Development Corporation in 1983.

24. Glass Bridge

Glenaffric Ave   Originally a section of Glengarnock Ave, renamed when the street was permanently divided at Manchester Rd in the 1960s.

Glengall   Margaret Lauretta, Countess of Glengall and wife of the 2nd Earl of Glengall, was the daughter of William Mellish. She inherited her father's considerable estate on the Isle of Dogs in 1834. Many places and buildings on the Island made use of the Glengall name.

Glengall Arms   Pub at 367 West Ferry Rd., built by Henry Bradshaw, a local grazier. The pub was bought in 1925 by the London Diocesan Fund for use as a priest's lodging and clubhouse in connection with St. Cuthbert's Church. It was acquired by the LCC in 1932 and demolished, together with nearby houses, for public housing developments (Arethusa House and other blocks of flats on Cahir St).

Glengall Rd./Grove   Glengall Grove (formerly Glengall Rd.) ran from West Ferry Rd. in the west to Manchester Rd. in the east, crossing. Millwall Docks, but when this access was stopped in 1963, the western half of Glengall Grove was renamed Tiller Rd.

Glengarnock Avenue   First named Church St (and running from Stebondale St to Saunder's Ness Rd.), it was renamed Newcastle St. in 1937 before being renamed Glengarnock Ave. See also *Glenaffric Ave.*

Glen Terrace   Named after the McGregor, Gow & Company's Glen Line which traded close by in West India Docks from 1879 until 1904.

Glenworth Avenue   Originally part of Billson St., the street was renamed at the end of the 1960s, with the building of the flats that blocked off Billson Rd. from Manchester Rd.

Great Eastern   Pub on the corner of West Ferry Rd. and British St. (now named Harbinger Rd.) that opened in 1860 and was destroyed by bombing during WWII. Its site is now occupied by the playground of Harbinger Primary School. Not to be confused with the similarly-named pub which was previously the Waterman's Arms.

25. Glengarnock Ave c1980

Globe Works   Rope works opened on East Ferry Rd. in 1881 by Hawkins & Tipson. The works were closed in the 1970s and demolished not long after. The Globe Rope Walk in Millwall Park follows the line of Hawkins & Tipson's ropewalk.

Greenwich Foot Tunnel   Built by the LCC and opened in 1901, the tunnel is 1,215 feet long. A section of the northern end was damaged by WWII bombing and was reinforced with concrete and steel.

Gun   First named the King & Queen (in 1722), the pub was also known as the Ramsgate Pink, and then Rose & Crown, before receiving its current name in 1771. The present building is 19th century.

26. Greenwich Foot Tunnel 1977

Gut House   In 1660, the Thames breached the river embankment (due to gravel quarrying in the vicinity), and after repairs there remained a large inland pond known as the Poplar Gut. The Gut House was built on the site of the breach, and did business until approximately 1810 when the pub had to make way for the City Canal. The landlord acquired land close by and built the first City Arms there.

Halyard House   A block of flats on the Samuda Estate which – like the neighbouring flats Pinnace, Reef, Yarrow, etc. – is named with a shipping theme. A halyard is the rope used to raise or lower sails.

Hammond House   Block of flats opened in Tiller Rd. (then Glengall Rd.) in 1938, and demolished in 2010. Named after 19th century property developer, George Hammond of Gravesend.

Harbinger Rd.   Originally named British St., renamed in 1930 by Poplar Borough Council due to there being another British St. in the council area (in Bow), and named after a clipper. The school was renamed at the same time.

Harbinger School   Built in 1872 to replace Millwall British School (and named as such on opening). Renamed Harbinger School in 1930.

Havannah St.   Named Thomas St. until 1875, Havannah was the Victorian English spelling of Havana, the capital of Cuba (a major source of sugar imports into the West India Docks).

27. Havannah St.

Hawkins & Tipson A rope and cable firm that opened its Globe Works on East Ferry Rd. in 1881. The works closed in 1971 and were demolished. The Globe Rope Walk in Millwall Park follows the line of Hawkins & Tipson's ropewalk.

Hedley House A block of flats on the Samuda Estate which – like the neighbouring flats Pinnace, Reef, Yarrow, etc. – is named with a shipping theme. Hedley was for a time the partner of shipbuilder Alfred Yarrow.

Hesperus Crescent A 1930-built housing crescent named after the Hesperus, a clipper ship on the Australian run.

Hibbert Gate George Hibbert (1757-1837) was a leading West India merchant and was instrumental in the creation of the West India Docks. He was appointed chairman at the first meeting of the West India Dock Company.

Hickin St. Created after WWII as part of the 1960s housing developments in the area.

Hookey Shore Informal name for a slipway between the rowing club and Ferry House which was used by barge breaker, John Hook.

St. Hubert's House Block of flats built on Janet St. by the Isle of Dogs Housing Society in 1936. Saint Hubertus or Hubert (c. 656–727 A.D.) is the patron saint of hunters, mathematicians, opticians, and metalworkers. Hunting motifs were employed in the decoration of the building.

Hutching's St. Named after A. J. Hutching & Company, wire-rope makers, of Hutching's Wharf.

Ingelheim Place/Cottages Ingelheim Place was a short street built by Weitzel and Knight in 1862, approximately at the location of the current Spindrift Rd. junction with West Ferry Rd. Ingelheim is a town on the Rhine, so perhaps the name was chosen by the German-born Weitzel.

28. Derelict Hawkins & Tipson Rope Walk c1979

Iron Church   The first St. Luke's Church (and school) was a temporary building, built in 1865. Due to its iron sheet construction, it was known as the Iron Church. When the permanent St. Luke's Church was opened in Strafford St., it functioned as a school only, being replaced by a permanent building in 1873.

Ironie, The   A scrap yard bounded by Janet St., Alpha Grove and Maria St. (where the entrance was). Apparently rarely used, it had more use as a playground for the local kids. In the early 1960s the scrap yard was cleared, and the site was tarmacked over and used as a football kick about pitch.

Ironmonger's Arms   The Ironmonger's Arms was built on West Ferry Rd. in 1860, approximately half way between The Vulcan and the Magnet & Dewdrop. It was closed in 1920.

Island Gardens   Opened in 1895 on land that was intended to be the site of large villas with a view of Greenwich. Not a commercial success, only one house was completed and the untended land became known as *Scrap Iron Park*, before the LCC invested in the creation of a public green space.

Islanders   Pub which opened in 1880 in Tooke St., and which was the first club house of Millwall FC. It was destroyed by bombing during WWII.

Isle of Dogs School   Originally named Millwall Glengall Rd. School, it opened in 1895 close to the baths. It later changed name when it became an 'open air school', whose philosophy was to provide maximum fresh air to children, to help prevent and combat tuberculosis (very prevalent before WWII). It was severely damaged during the war, and not rebuilt.

Isle House   Built as Dock Master's residence in Cold Harbour in 1826 by the West India Dock Company.

Janet St.   Originally named Jane St. (changed in 1876), the street disappeared on creation of the Barkantine Estate in the 1960s. Pronounced as *Janette St.* by local residents.

29. Islanders pub (right) on Tooke St.

St. John's Church Built in 1872 on Roserton St. (at location of present-day Island House Community Centre on Castalia Square), built in 1872 and damaged beyond use by WWII bombing. It was never repaired and was demolished in the 1950s.

30. St. John's Church

St. John's Community Centre Built on Glengall Grove in 1981, on the site of a former entrance to the Transport Yard in the Mudchute.

St. John's House Sheltered housing built in 1974 on Pier St. by the Isle of Dogs Housing Association.

St. John's Park Opened in 1966 as St. John's Recreation Ground, named after the former church and parish, it was renamed St. John's Park in 1989 after extensive redevelopment.

St. John's School School associated with (and close to) St. John's Church. Built at the same time as the church, it was also damaged beyond use in WWII.

Johnson Draw Dock Named after Henry and Augustus William Johnson, owners of extensive works on Ferry St. in the mid-19th century (Henry was also responsible for building the Lord Nelson pub).

Johnson St. The original name of the section of Ferry St. that runs from Johnson Draw Dock to Manchester Rd. The name was changed in c1938.

Jubilee Chapel Early name for the Cubitt Town Primitive Methodist Church.

Jubilee Crescent The crescent and its houses were built in 1935 by local ship repairers R. & H. Green & Silley Weir Ltd, to provide affordable homes for retirees of the firm. It was named after Jubilee Chapel.

Judkin St.   Renamed from Judkins St. in 1911, it was laid out by the Millwall Dock Company in the 1880s. Possibly named for a dock company official of the time.

Kedge House   A kedge is a light anchor that is dropped overboard and then used to draw the vessel towards it. Kedge House was built on Tiller Rd. in the later 1960s.

Kelson House   The kelson or keelson is the member which, particularly in a wooden vessel, lies parallel with its keel but above the transverse members such as timbers, in order to provide the keel more stiffness. Perhaps this name was chosen to reflect the 'scissor' design of flats in Kelson House (opened in 1967).

Killoran House   Block of flats built in the mid-1960s and named after a ship that frequently used Millwall Docks.

Kimberley House   Block of flats built in the mid-1960s and named after a former warden of Dockland Settlement on East Ferry Rd.

King's Arms   Public house that was present in the late 1800s at the west end of Timothy's Wharf (close to the present-day Arnhem Place). At the time, access to the river was provided by the adjacent King's Arms Stairs.

Kingdon House   Block of flats opened in the mid-1960s and named after a popular and long-serving former vicar of St. John's Church.

Kingfield St.   Laid out in the 1840s as part of the Cubitt Town development. It remained undeveloped until the 20th century when the council built houses on it as a part of its Kingfield Estate.

Kingfisher Court   Named after the gunboat, HMS Kingfisher, launched from Yarrow's Yard.

Kingsbridge   Never an official name, Kingsbridge was the iron swing bridge at the Millwall Docks entrance lock near the Kingsbridge Arms.

31. Kingfield St.

Kingsbridge Arms Pub on the southern corner of Crews St. and West Ferry Rd. Opened in 1839, it closed in 2004 and was demolished shortly afterwards.

Knighthead Point One of the four tall blocks on the Barkantine estate, opened c1970. The four blocks, in combination with The Quarterdeck, are meant to represent a ship. A knighthead is either of two timbers rising from the keel of a sailing ship and supporting the inner end of the bowsprit.

Launch St. Street created in the 1950s as a part of the post-war development of the Glengall Grove area.

John Lenanton Timber firm that started business on the former Batson's Wharf in 1864. For the next century, the firm expanded to include more wharves in the area. In 1971 they created more room by buying St. Luke's School. The yard closed in the 1990s.

Locke, Lancaster & Co. The lead producers and merchants, John Locke and Co was established in 1790. After a series of mergers, the company was known in 1892 as Locke, Lancaster & Co, Lead Merchants & Desilverisers. In 1895, the company acquired the business and factory of the Millwall Lead Co (formerly Pontifex and Wood). A 1924 the company formed a consortium with other firms. The resulting partnership was named Associated Lead Manufacturers.

London Tavern Public house built in 1860 on the northern corner of Glengall Rd. and Manchester Rd. by Charles Davis (also responsible for building the Pier Tavern and Manchester Arms). It carried on doing business until 1954, after which it survived into the 60s as a one-storey shell.

Lord Nelson The Lord Nelson was built in 1855 and is one the few remaining original Island pubs that is still doing business. In 1886, Millwall Rovers left their Millwall headquarters at The Islanders pub in Tooke St., and moved to the Nelson. For the next 4 years the team played at a ground behind the pub (where Manchester Grove is now located).

Lead St. A short street of terraced houses built in the 1860s opposite the lead works. It later provided access to the works' football pitch between West East Ferry Rd., East Ferry Rd. and Chapel House St. Lockesfield Place follows the route of Lead St.

32. Kingsbridge Arms

Lingard House   Block of flats built in the 1960s on Marshfield St., and named after a ship that frequently used the docks.

Llandovery House   Block of flats built in the 1960s on Roffey St., and named after a ship that frequently used the docks.

London Yard   Created in 1857 by a partnership of Robert Baillie, Joseph Westwood and James Campbell, the yard was named after London St., which originally gave access to the yard.

St. Luke's Church   The first St. Luke's church (which was also a school) was on the west side of West Ferry Rd., the later location of St. Luke's School. In 1873, a permanent church and vicarage were built on Strafford St. Seriously damaged during WWII, the church was demolished in 1960, while congregations continued in a 'temporary' building, which itself was demolished in 2014. A new church and community centre will be built on the spot.

St. Luke's School   The first dedicated St. Luke's School was built in 1873 on West Ferry Rd. (by the same firm who built St. Luke's vicarage on Strafford St). In 1971, Lenanton's timber firm acquired the school and its land in order to expand their business, and the school moved to the former Cubitt Town school premises on Saunders Ness Rd.

Luralda   Luralda, manufacturers of tea chests, took over the former Sapon Soaps works on Saunders Ness Rd. (next to the Island Gardens) in the late 1920s. Later specialising in all sorts of plywood packaging, they occupied Luralda Wharf until the 1980s.

Maconochies   Maconochie's Wharf (formerly Northumberland Wharf), off West Ferry Rd. near the Ship public house, was occupied from about 1896 by Maconochie Brothers. Maconochies were wholesale provision merchants and manufacturers of pickles, potted meat and fish, jam, marmalade and other preserved foods. A family business until the 1920s, Maconochies was wound up in the early 1970s, but the firm had already left the Island some years before.

33. St. Luke's Church

Magnet & Dewdrop (1850-1995) Built in 1850, one of three pubs built on land belonging to the Ironmonger's Company with an ironmongery-themed name (the other two being the Vulcan and the Ironmonger's Arms). It was renamed the Telegraph in 1985, and closed in 1995. It is now occupied by flats.

Malabar St. Originally named Charles St., its name was changed in 1891, matching the change to West Indian names of other streets in the area (Cuba, Havannah, Tobago, etc).

Managers St. Street created in 1885 between Cold Harbour and Preston's Rd. Named after the Managers of the Metropolitan Asylums Board. The board was established in 1867 under Poor Law legislation, to deal with London's sick poor. It was wound up in 1930, its functions being transferred to the London County Council.

G. W. Mancell Steel company at the end of Cahir St. and Harbinger Rd.

34. Malabar St. in 1906.

Macquarie Way   A 1930-built housing crescent named after the Macquarie, a clipper ship on the Australian run.

Manchester Arms   Pub built by Charles Davis (who also built the Pier Tavern and London Tavern) on the southern corner of Samuda St. and Manchester Rd. in 1858. It was badly damaged by WWII bombing, and demolished shortly afterwards.

Manchester Grove   Street built in 1926, with similar designs to that of the nearby Chapel House St.

Manchester Rd.   Road built in the 1840s by William Cubitt as part of his Cubitt Town development.

Manilla St.   Original named Alfred St. (after Alfred Batson), its name was changed in 1875, matching the change to West Indian names of other streets in the area (Cuba, Havannah, Tobago, etc).

Maple House   Along with other blocks on the estate, named after a tree sort in reference to the timber import in Millwall Docks. Demolished in 1988.

Mechanics Arms   Pub at the West Ferry Rd. end of Spratley's Row (a narrow street, starting approximately

Maria St.   Street laid out in the 1860s. The street disappeared on creation of the Barkantine Estate in the 1960s.

Marsh St. I   Original name of Tobago St., changed in 1876.

Marsh St. II   Running between Harbinger Rd. and Cahir St., behind Harbinger School, Marsh St. used to extend further north.

Marshfield St.   Created in 1860 as a part of the new Cubitt Town.

Mast House Terrace   A tidal dock, known as Drunken Dock, was later used as a mast pond when a mast house was built on the riverfront (in the late 1700s). A rough path from the 19th century Mast House Cottages to Totnes Cottages later became known as Mast House Terrace. The dock had been filled-in by this time.

Maudslay House   Block of flats on Tiller Rd., named after the Blackwall Engineering company, Maudslay, Sons & Field opposite Byng St. and running up towards the river). The pub opened in 1818 and was documented as still open in 1920, but it is not known when it closed.

Mellish St.   Shadwell butcher, Peter Mellish, owned several acres of land in Millwall in the 1770s which were later inherited by his son William. On William's death in 1833, the land was inherited by his daughter Margaret, who later married the Earl of Glengall.

Michigan House   Block of flats on the Millwall Estate near Kingsbridge, named after the SS Michigan, a transatlantic cargo ship which was a frequent visitor to Millwall Docks. Michigan House was built in 1960, much later than the other blocks on the estate, Montrose House and Montcalm House.

Midship Point   One of the four tall blocks on the Barkantine estate, opened c1970. The four blocks, in combination with The Quarterdeck, are meant to represent a ship. The midship is the portion of a ship between the bow and the stern.

St. Mildred's House   Originally, an institute for poor girls set up in 1897 in the former Millwall Dock Club behind St. Paul's Church on West Ferry Rd. In the 1960s, St. Mildred's House moved to new premises on Castalia Square.

Millwall   A man-made river embankment (usually earthen with timber reinforcement) was in the past frequently referred to as a *wall*. Mill Wall, originally two words, was the name given to the Island's western Thames embankment due to its many windmills.

Millwall Central School   Opened in 1928 on land between Maria St. and Janet St., sharing space with the already present, so-called Janet St. (Mentally Defective) Council School. Both schools were damaged by bombing during WWII and closed in 1945.

35. Mellish St. street party

Millwall Cinema   Located at 221 West Ferry Rd., about half way between Glengall Rd. (now Tiller Rd.) and the Millwall Dock entrance at Kingsbridge. It had 1000 seats and 100 standing places.

The cinema only lasted from 1912-1915, its business being terminally-affected by the outbreak of WWI. But the building - which started life as an engineering workshop, complete with corrugated iron roof - continued to be used until 1963, lastly by the iron and steel firm, G. Robinson & Sons.

Millwall Cooperage   Located in the middle of what is now Hesperus Crescent (and the main reason for the circular form of the street – the council could not afford to buy the cooperage out at the time, so they built round it).

Millwall Docks   Opened in 1867 and consisting of a west-east Outer Dock connected to a south-north Inner Dock. It was connected to the river via an entrance lock at Kingsbridge. Only later would it be connected to West India Docks via the so-called Millwall Cutting (after which the Kingsbridge entrance lost its usefulness and ceased to be used).

Despite being among the most modern and efficient docks in the world, Millwall Docks could not compete with container-handling docks further down river and closed in 1980.

Millwall Dock Station   Railway station on the London and Blackwall Railway line, built in 1871 on East Ferry Rd. and never reopened after the 1926 General Strike. Crossharbour DLR station is built more or less on the site of the former station.

Millwall Docks Tavern & Hotel   A grand hotel and pub, built in 1869 next to the Millwall Dock entrance just north of Kingsbridge. It was destroyed in the blitz.

Millwall FC   First known as Millwall Rovers when it was started in 1885 by workers from Morton's factory and when its club house was in the Islanders pub in Tooke St. The team proceeded to have four grounds on the Island, changing its name to Millwall Athletic at one stage, before moving to New Cross in 1910. Its Island grounds were located at (a) waste ground off Tiller Rd. (modern name), (b) behind the Lord Nelson pub, where Manchester Grove now is, (c) an athletics ground on the site of the present-day Asda, and (d) in Millwall Park, on the site of the future George Green's school playing field.

Millwall Independent Chapel Independent Chapel at 127A West Ferry Rd. Built in 1817, it was the first place of worship on the Island since the medieval chapel of St. Mary. The church closed in 1908, but the building continued to be used for other purposes until its demolition in the 1950s.

Millwall Iron Works A conglomeration of different companies (in different combinations at different times) that grew to be the largest iron and shipbuilding works on the Island, employing at one stage up to 5000 men.

The original works were created by William Fairbairn in 1836, on West Ferry Rd., close to the site of the later Ship public house. John Scott Russell took over the site in 1848, and it later became the construction site of the Great Eastern. This venture bankrupted Russell, and in 1859 the works were taken over by C. J. Mare & Company, and then the Millwall Iron Works Ship Building & Graving Docks Company Ltd.

By 1888, this company had collapsed, and the works (which had expanded to be on both sides of West Ferry Rd.) were split up into different parcels, one of which was taken over by the Burrell's company.

Millwall Park Until well into the 20th century, the land that is now known as Millwall Park belonged to the Port of London Authority who had plans to one day extend the Millwall Docks across the east of the Island to the Thames. For this reason, the land was not developed and was mostly used for pasture.

In 1919, London County Council bought the land and created Millwall Recreation Ground, known for years by locals as *New Park*. In 1925, the park was complemented with an open air swimming pool (close to the end of Billson St).

36. Millwall Park paddling pool, c1972

Millwall Seamen's Institute & Rest   Built in 1891 by the British and Foreign Sailors' Society to provide accommodation (and a temperate alternative to pubs) for visiting sailors. It was location on a triangle of land between the Millwall Docks entrance at Kingsbridge and West Ferry Rd. It was demolished in the 1930s.

Millwall Wharf   The lease on the wharf south of London Yard was acquired in 1875 by the Millwall Wharf & Warehouse Company, who rented it to wharfinger and lighterman, James Cook. He built an extensive range of warehouses, some of which are still standing along the riverfront (and are Grade II listed). Cook & Company occupied Millwall Wharf until the 1960s, when the leases were taken over by Cory Associated Wharves Ltd.

Moiety Rd.   A *moiety* is defined as *one of two approximately equal parts.* Moiety Rd. was created by William Tooke in 1817, and it has been suggested he meant this road to be a boundary between the residential and industrial parts of his land.

Montcalm House   Block of flats on the Millwall Estate near Kingsbridge, named after the Canadian Pacific SS Montcalm, a transatlantic liner/cargo-ship which was a frequent visitor to Millwall Docks.

Montague L. Meyer   Timber firm that operated from the 1930s on the south quay of the Millwall Outer Dock, with an entrance close to the Kingsbridge Arms, on land leased from the dock company. The yard closed at the same time as the Millwall Docks in the early 1980s.

Montfort House   Block of flats built in the mid-1960s and named after a ship that frequented Millwall Docks.

Montrose House   Block of flats on the Millwall Estate near Kingsbridge, named after the Canadian Pacific SS Montrose, a transatlantic liner/cargo-ship which was a frequent visitor to Millwall Docks.

37. Montrose

38. Montague Meyer

Morton's J. T. Morton was an Aberdeen provision's merchant who started his business in 1849. In 1872 he opened a factory in the north of Millwall, between West Ferry Rd. and the river. Workers from his company famously founded Millwall Football Club in the 1880's. After his death in 1897, his sons took over and the firm became C & E Morton Ltd.

The business expanded to be one of the largest employers on the Island, with factories on both side of West Ferry Rd. north of Cuba St., and one in Cubitt Town, near London Yard. In 1945, Morton's was taken over by Beechams.

Mudchute (aka Muddy) The name derives from it being the former dumping ground for mud dredged from the Millwall Docks which had to be regularly dredged to prevent silting up. A novel, pneumatic device was employed which pumped the liquefied mud through a pipe over East Ferry Rd. (close to the George pub), dumping it on the other side.

39. Mudchute c1977

Napier Yard Marine engineer David Napier laid out his yard in 1836, approximately opposite Harbinger School. The yard and its works were destroyed by fire in 1853, and the land was taken over by John Scott Russell, for use in the building of the Great Eastern.

Nelson House House built at 3 Cold Harbour in 1820, and received the Nelson House name in the 1880s. Despite local tradition, there is no evidence to support the house ever having an association with Lord Nelson.

Newcastle Arms Pub built by Cubitt & Co. in 1853 next to Newcastle Draw Dock, it was renamed the Waterman's Arms by Daniel Farson in 1962. In 2011, it was renamed the Great Eastern.

Newcastle St. Formerly named Church St., this street ran from Stebondale St. to Saunders Ness Rd. It was renamed Glengarnock Avenue in 1937.

Newcastle Draw Dock Grade II listed draw dock on Saunders Ness Rd., constructed by William Cubitt in the 1840s.

Newty Drainage ditch that ran round the south and south-eastern edges of the Mudchute, named after the many newts residing in the water. An exciting and unforgettable place to play for generations of Island kids.

40. Newcastle Draw Dock

New Union Close Named after, and built on the site of, New Union Wharf. Formerly the site of Yarrow's shipbuilding yard, New Union Wharf received its new name when it was taken over by the Union Lighterage Company of Blackwall.

Nightingale Court Named after the gunboat, HMS Nightingale, launched from Yarrow's Yard in 1897.

Normandy House Block of flats named after a ship which frequently visited the docks.

North Greenwich Station Railway station on the London and Blackwall Railway line, built in 1871 on Johnson St. (renamed Ferry St. in 1938, the section running from Manchester Rd. to Johnson Draw Dock). The station closed in 1926 and was later used as a storage yard by a lighterage company. The first Island Gardens DLR station and the Poplar and Blackwall District Rowing Club were late built on the site.

North Pole Pub built in the 1860s on Manilla St. (at that time, the corner of Manilla St. and Alpha Rd.). The pub closed in 2014 and is scheduled for demolition.

41. North Pole

42. St. Paul's Church and Pisa Cathedral

Oak House   Along with other blocks on the estate, named after a tree sort in reference to the timber import in Millwall Docks.

Olliffe St.   Street next to the former Cubitt Arms. Presumably so named by William Cubitt after his daughter, Laura, married Sir Joseph Francis Olliffe.

Ord St.   The main road between the later City Arms and Cuba St. Became part of West Ferry Rd. in 1875.

Osborne House   Island Gardens was originally intended to be a 'plantation' with large villas. Only one was fully built and occupied. It was named Thames House, then renamed Dresden House (or Hall), and eventually Osborne House. In 1895, Osborne House was purchased by the LCC and became a library. Later it became a tea house for the Island Gardens. It was demolished in the 1950s.

Ovex Close   Named after Ovex Wharf, the name given to the wharf off Stewart St. by the Ovex Fuel Company 1910. The wharf was later taken over the Rye Arc Welding Company, who operated there until the 1970s.

Parsonage St.   Laid out by William Cubitt in the 1850s as a part of his Cubitt Town development, the street was not fully built upon due to the financial crisis of the late 1860s. In fact, it was the 1920s before the street was filled with houses, as part of Poplar Borough Council's *Kingfield Estate* development. Many houses were damaged during WWII, and these were replaced by supposedly temporary Orlit Houses, all but one of which are still standing.

St. Paul's Church   St. Paul's Presbyterian church - opened in 1860 specifically for the many Scottish workers who had migrated to the Island - was designed to look like the west front of Pisa Cathedral. The resemblance is very clear. Today, St. Paul's is the performing Arts Centre, 'The Space'.

Pier St.   Named for Cubitt Town Pier, constructed in 1857 by William Cubitt. Pier St. originally crossed Manchester Rd., running up to the river, but it disappeared under the expansion of Millwall Wharf. The section of Pier St. which is north of Betty May Gray House was originally part of Stebondale St.

Pier Head Cottages   Built in 1875 along the north side of the Millwall Dock entrance lock at Kingsbridge, and intended for senior dock workers.

Pier Tavern Pub built by Charles Davis (who also built the London Tavern and the Manchester Arms) on the corner of Pier St. and Manchester Rd. in 1863 and converted to a restaurant in March 2013. The restaurant has since closed.

43. The Pier Tavern

Pin and Cotter The informal and more frequently used name for the Union Arms.

Pinnace House A block of flats on the Samuda Estate which – like the neighbouring flats, Reef, Yarrow, etc – is named with a shipping theme. A pinnace is light boat which was carried aboard larger boats or ships, mainly used as a tender.

Plevna St. Street created during the Cubitt Town development. Named after the Siege of Plevna, a battle during the Russo-Turkish War (1877–78).

Pontifex & Wood Edward and William Pontifex and J. Wood were iron founders, engineers, millwrights, copper smiths, refrigerator and boiler makers, whose firm opened its works on the Island in 1843. Renamed Millwall Lead Co, it was acquired in 1895 by a conglomeration that included Locke, Lancaster & Co.

Poplar, Blackwall & District Rowing Club
Founded by lightermen in 1854, it is one of the oldest rowing clubs in Great Britain. Its first club house (and boat storage place) was the nearby Princess of Wales pub. The current boat house was built in the late 1960s.

44. Rowing club members off Greenwich. Island Gardens, Galleon House and Luralda Wharf are visible over the water.

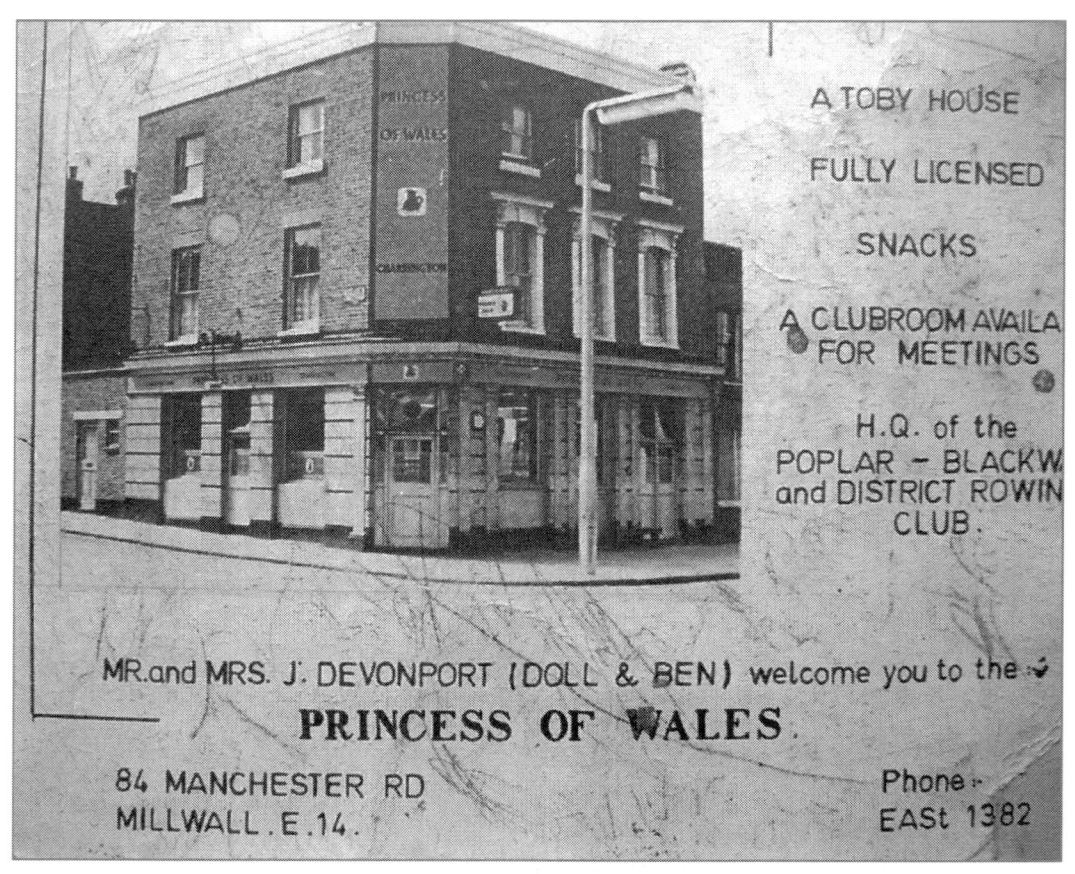

A TOBY HOUSE

FULLY LICENSED

SNACKS

A CLUBROOM AVAILA
FOR MEETINGS

H.Q. of the
POPLAR - BLACKW
and DISTRICT ROWIN
CLUB.

MR. and MRS. J. DEVONPORT (DOLL & BEN) welcome you to the

PRINCESS OF WALES

84 MANCHESTER RD
MILLWALL . E .14.

Phone -
EASt 1382

45. Princess of Wales, also known as Macs

Poplar Dry Dock   A former slipway off Saunders Ness Rd. (close to Christ Church) that was converted into a dry dock in 1870. Later, the yard was taken over by Sternols. A memory of the dry dock is visible in the form of a pond between Storer's Quay and Caledonia Wharf.

Potter's Ferry   A ferry has existed between the south of the Island (where the Ferry House is) and Greenwich since medieval times. In the early 1600s it was first referred to as Potter's Ferry, a name that remained in use long after. The dry dock on the site was known as Potter's Dry Dock until the end of the 20th century.

Powis Rd.   Charles Powis developed the site opposite St. Paul's Church in 1873, creating at the same time a road to the river known as Powis Rd. When the wharf was taken over by Le Bas and was renamed Cyclops Wharf, the road was renamed Cyclops Place.

Preston's Rd.   Original name, New Rd., changed in 1907, when named after Robert Preston, a captain with the East India Company, who in 1783 came into possession of a large estate which extended from Blackwall to south of Cold Harbour (the street, Cold Harbour and the houses on it were not part of the estate).

Pride of the Isle   Pub on the corner of Havannah St. and Cheval St., built in 1846. It figured largely in the 1960s film *Sparrows Can't Sing*, although it was renamed The Red Lion in the film. It was demolished in the 1960s to make room for the Barkantine Estate.

Prince Alfred Formerly a beer house on the corner of Tobago St. and Manilla St. in 1906. It was seriously damaged (and closed) by WWII bombing.

Prince of Wales   Pub on the riverfront at Folly Wall, built in 1859. It was fairly run down by WWI and destroyed by WWII bombing.

Princess of Wales Built in 1862 on the corner of Manchester Rd. and Barque St., the pub was more commonly known as Macs, a very long lasting reference to its first landlord, William Patrick McMahon.   It was closed at the end of the 1960's in connection with the demolition of a long stretch of housing on Manchester Rd. to make room for George Green's school.

Quarterdeck The central, small shopping area of the Barkantine Estate, opened c1970. In combination with the four tower blocks on the estate, meant to represent a ship. The quarterdeck is a raised deck behind the main mast of a sailing ship. Traditionally it was where the captain commanded his vessel and where the ship's colours were kept. This led to it being used as the main ceremonial and reception area on board, and the word is still used to refer to such an area on a ship or even in naval establishments on land.

Queen Pub built in 1855 on the sharp corner of East Ferry Rd. and Manchester Rd. In the 1980s it was called Queens for a while, and finally Queen of the Isle from 1995. It was demolished in 2004.

Rawalpindi House Block of flats built in 1947 in Mellish St., and constructed according to Orlit prefabricated housing methods (the same method used for post-war housing still present on Parsonage St. and Billson St). The block was named after the merchant ship *Rawalpindi*, which was sunk by enemy action during WWII. Now demolished.

Reef House Block of flats on the 1960s Samuda Estate.

Regent Dock Rd. Former public way to the river north of Regent Dry Dock, closed by Lenanton's when their expansion consumed the road.

Regent Dry Dock Opened on the riverfront opposite Byng St. in 1817. The dock was eventually filled in by Lenanton's in 1932 after they had taken over the yard as part of their own expansion.

J. & G. Rennie John Rennie (senior) was chief engineer at the West India Docks from 1809 to 1821. His sons John and George Rennie continued his work, and also started their own marine engineering business in Millwall. The Rennies were responsible for the design and building of many dock buildings and works, including the Rum Quay Shed, Ledger Building, Cannon Workshops, and some lock bridges, impounding stations, cranes and engines.

46. The Queen (of the Isle)

Robert Burns Pub opened in West Ferry Rd. in 1853, presumably to take advantage of the custom generated by the neighbouring construction of the SS Great Eastern (launched in 1858). The pub closed in 1991.

Robert St. Named after local landowner Robert Batson. Name changed to Cuba St. in 1875.

Robin Court Named after the gunboat, HMS Robin, launched from Yarrow's Yard in 1897.

Rodney House Block of flats built on the West Ferry Estate in Cahir St., and opened in 1935. Like other flats on the estate, it was named after a Merchant Navy training ship.

Roffey House Block of flats built on Roffey St. (at the same time as Cubitt House) and demolished in 1988.

Roffey St. Laid out by the Millwall Dock Company in the 1880s. Possibly named for a dock company official of the time.

Roserton St. Originally planned to be named Lavenham St., Roserton St. was laid out in c1860. Name origin unknown.

Rugless House Block of flats at the north end of East Ferry Rd., opened in 1952, and named after Alderman J. J. Rugless, one of the 30 Poplar Borough Councillors imprisoned in 1921 after a protest against an unfair rating system.

Rum Quay Much of the south quay of the West India Import (South) Dock had specialised warehouses to handle and store rum imports. The warehouses were destroyed by WWII bombing.

Saddler's Park Green space formerly between Manchester Rd., Samuda St., Stewart St. and Davis St. It, and most of the housing around it, were destroyed during WWII bombing.

Salford House Block of flats in Seyssel St., built in 1962 as part of the Manchester Estate. Like other blocks in the estate, named after an area of Greater Manchester.

47. Robert Burns

Samuda Estate   Named after the Samuda Brothers Shipbuilding Company whose original yard was built on the site c1850. The brothers were Jacob and Joseph Samuda. After the death of Jacob in an accident on the Thames, the firm was run solely by Joseph d'Aguilar Samuda (1813–1885), civil engineer and politician.

The company occupied the yard until 1893, but the name Samuda's Yard existed until after WWII (during which the yard was seriously damaged). The land was purchased by the LCC in the 1950s for the creation of the Samuda Estate.

Sandpiper Court   Named after the gunboat, HMS Sandpiper, launched from Yarrow's Yard.

Saunders Ness Rd.   Amongst other definitions, a *ness* is a headland or promontory, and Saunders Ness is one of the earliest documented Island place, mentioned on Robert Adam's 1588 map, *Thamesis Descriptio*. Its location corresponds to the riverfront just north of Newcastle Draw Dock, on Saunders Ness Rd. (named Wharf Rd. until 1937).

Schooner St.   See *Ship St.*

J. Scott Russell   Scottish shipbuilder whose firm built the Great Eastern. The building and launching of the ship bankrupted Russell, and his shipbuilding yard was in operation on West Ferry Rd. from 1853 to only 1857. Russell laid the foundation stone of St. Paul's church (now The Space arts centre) in 1859.

Scoulding House   Block of flats opened in Mellish St. in 1967 and named after John Thomas ('Tom') Scoulding (c.1875-1960), trade unionist and Labour Party politician. Scoulding was an official of the Amalgamated Society of Watermen, Lightermen and Bargemen, Mayor of West Ham in 1931-1932, and was appointed by the government to the Port of London Authority.

Seacon   Express Wharf (south of Lenanton's) was owned by Freight Express who merged with the shipping and freight-forwarding agency Seacon to form Freight Express-Seacon Ltd in 1973. The wharf was redeveloped, and two large open sheds were constructed to handle steel cargoes.

48. Snowdrift lorry on Saunders Ness Rd.

Seven Mills School   Primary school opened on the Barkantine Estate in 1968. The name is derived from a 1703 map by Gascoyne, which shows seven windmills along the riverfront. However, there were less or more windmills at various times in history.

Seyssel St.   Named after the Asphalte de Seyssel Company of Thames Embankment, which in 1861 developed a wharf close by (later named Pyrimont Wharf).

Ship Pub   In the 1830s, houses along West Ferry Rd., close to Maconochie's Wharf, were built. Two were later rebuilt as The Ship public house, which is still doing business.

Ship St.   One of three streets between Saunders Ness Rd. (then Wharf Rd.) and Manchester Rd. laid out c1860 and named with a sailing ship theme (the other two being Brig St. and Barque St). The street was later renamed Schooner St.

Skeggs House   Block of flats opened in Glengall Grove in 1956, named after J. B. Skeggs OBE, Town Clerk of Poplar from 1915 to 1922.

Snowdon, Sons & Co.   Motor oil manufacturers who had works on Lowe's Wharf (situated between Kingsbridge Arms and the Millwall Outer Dock entrance) until well after WWII. Their site was cleared in the mid-1980s.

Spinnaker House   One of the last Barkantine Estate housing developments, built between Byng St. and Strafford St. in at the end of the 1970s. A spinnaker is a type of sail which is employed at the front of a boat.

Spring Gardens Place   Small row of cottages off the west end of Janet St.

Stebondale St.   A reference to *Stebonheath*, an early version of the name, Stepney (of which the Isle of Dogs was a part). The street was virtually destroyed during the blitz.

49. Stebondale St.

50. Tate & Lyle

Stewart St. Named after John Stewart who established his Blackwall Iron Works here in the 1850s for the manufacture of marine engines.

Stewart St. Pumping Station The first storm-water pumping station, designed to relieve over overcharged sewers, was built on Stewart St. in 1888. Continually extended and revised over the following century, the striking new pumping station was built in 1988.

Strafford St. Named after John Byng, Viscount Enfield and Earl of Strafford in 1847, grandson of 18th century Island landowner Robert Byng.

Strattondale St. Named after William Stratton, from whom William Cubitt leased 8 acres for his Cubitt Town development in 1850.

Strattondale St. Library Opened in 1905, its construction was financed largely by Scottish American philanthropist, Andrew Carnegie. It replaced the public library at Osborne House in Island Gardens.

Stuart's Granolithic Stone A large site between Island Baths and the Capewell Horse Nail Factory (site of future glass bridge entrance) was acquired in 1900 as the London works of the Scottish company, Stuart's Granolithic Stone Company Ltd. Stuart's head office remained at the works until 1958, when it was transferred to Harrow. The works closed in 1962. The site was briefly a road-haulage depot and was then redeveloped for public housing.

Talia House Block of flats on the late 1960s Barkantine Estate.

Tate & Lyle Sugar manufacturers Tate & Lyle acquired their Millwall site (at the east end of Janet and Malabar Streets) in 1964 from Brown and Polson, who had purchased what was previously named Broadway Works from George Clark & Son in 1956. The works closed in the early 90s.

Thermopylae Gate A 1930s-built housing crescent named after the Thermopylae, a clipper ship on the Australian run.

Thomas St. Original name of Havannah St., changed in 1875.

Thorne House Block of flats in Glengall Grove opened in 1956 and named after Poplar Borough Librarian, William Benson Thorne (1878-1966). He was the first President (in 1908) of the Library Assistants' Association and enjoyed a long and distinguished career in his field.

Tideway House   Block of flats built in the late 1960s as part of the Barkantine Estate development. *The Tideway* is a name given to that part of the Thames that is subject to tides (i.e. everything downstream of Teddington Lock).

Tiller Rd.   Glengall Grove (formerly Glengall Rd.) ran from West Ferry Rd. in the west to Manchester Rd. in the east. The road crossed Millwall Docks, but when this vehicular access was stopped in 1963, the western half of Glengall Grove was renamed Tiller Rd. A tiller, in the nautical sense, is the lever attached to the rudder and used for steering.

Tobago St.   Originally named George St., its name was changed in 1876, matching the change to West Indian names of other streets in the area (Cuba, Havannah, Manilla, etc).

Tooke Arms   This pub was present by 1853, at the corner of West Ferry Rd. and Janet St. It was rebuilt at a location approximately 40 yards further along West Ferry Rd. in 1970.

Tooke St.   Named after Thomas Tooke, an 18th century 'citizen and draper' who acquired a 20 acre estate in Millwall as a consequence of his marriage to the daughter of Richard Chevall. His son, Charles Chevall Tooke, was the first to sell house-building plots on the estate, in the 1840s. The street disappeared on creation of the Barkantine Estate in the 1960s.

A WATNEY HOUSE

FULLY LICENSED

LUNCHEONS AND
SNACKS

—

Telephone :-
EASt 5910

—

MR. & MRS. L.R. MOSS. (Roy. & Kay.) welcome you to

THE TOOKE ARMS

165, WEST FERRY ROAD. MILLWALL. E 14

51. The Tooke Arms

52. Tooke St. on VE Day

Topmast Point   One of the four tower blocks on the Barkantine estate, opened c1970. The four blocks, in combination with The Quarterdeck, are meant to represent a ship. Traditional ship masts are not single spars, but are made up of two or even three spars. The mast above the lower mast (aka mizzen, main or fore) is known as the topmast.

Torrington Arms   Built in 1856 by the Spratley family from Stepney. It had ceased to be a pub by 1909. Named after the third son of Admiral George Byng, 1st Viscount Torrington.

Torrington Causeway   Road through the former Torrington Yard (across West Ferry Rd. from Strafford St) providing access to the river.

Totnes Cottages   A short terrace of houses built in approximately 1860 behind West Ferry Rd. near the Vulcan, and running up towards Britannia Dock. Named by one of the builders, who came from Totnes.

Triton House   Block of flats opened in 1933, and named after a Merchant Navy training ship.

John Tucker House   Block of flats in Mellish St., built in the 1960s. Named after John Tucker who was mayor of Poplar from 1964-1965.

53. John Tucker, the last Mayor of Poplar

Union Arms   Built in the 1830s, and better known by locals as the Pin & Cotter, the pub was still doing business in 1960. Its postal address was 102 West Ferry Rd., but it was some yards up Union Rd.

Union Docks   For close to 100 years from 1883, all the land between The Walls and the river was occupied by Union Docks, and consisted of a combination of dry docks, tidal docks and slipways.

Union Rd.   A short, narrow road from West Ferry Rd. to the river, became part of Mellish St. in 1937.

Urmston House   Block of flats in Pier St., built in 1962 as part of the Manchester Estate. Like other blocks in the estate, named after an area of Greater Manchester.

Valiant House   Block of flats named after a ship which frequently visited the docks.

Vulcan   The Vulcan pub was established by 1882, its name reflecting the business of the landowners, the Ironmonger's Company. The pub closed in 1992 and the building now houses a restaurant.

Walls, The   The local name for the few hundred yards of curving West Ferry Rd. (Bridge Rd. until 1937) at its Limehouse end. Its curve corresponded to the river wall around the Poplar Breach.

On the east side of the road was a high wall separating it from the docks, and on the west side was a mixture of walls and fences separating it from riverside firms and dry docks. The Walls were demolished as a consequence of the new Canary Wharf developments.

Warspite House Block of flats built on the West Ferry Estate in Cahir St., and opened in 1935. Like other flats on the estate, it was named after a Merchant Navy training ship.

Waterman's Arms I (1813-1920)   In 1813 George Henn, a ship-chandler, built a beer house, later called the Waterman's or Watermen's Arms on the south-west corner of Cuba St. and West Ferry Rd. It survived until at least 1921.

Waterman's Arms II See *Newcastle Arms*

54. The Walls

Waterman's Lodge   Beer house set up in 1870 in a house in Totnes Terrace.

Welcome Institute   An institute set up in the late 1800s at 333 West Ferry Rd. Its main purpose was to provide support, classes and hot meals to factory girls. The institute moved to new premises in East Ferry Rd. in 1905 (the premises were later taken over by the Dockland Settlement).

Western Granaries   Built in 1884, the three Western Granaries were situated in the west most part of Millwall Dock, bordering on Alpha Rd. One of the granaries later formed the basis of the Broadway Works, used by G. Clark & Sons. The land was later used by Tate & Lyle.

West Ferry Rd.   Originally a toll road, the West Ferry Rd. was the main road to/from the Greenwich ferry at the south of the Island. The section between Cuba St. and the City Arms was known until 1875 as Ord St. The section from the City Arms to Garford St. was known until 1937 as Bridge Rd.

West India Dock Pier   Constructed at the end of Cuba St. in 1875, the pier was destroyed by WWII bombing, but was rebuilt and reopened in 1950 in time for use as part of the Festival of Britain (specifically, for visitors travelling to/from the Lanbury Estate in Poplar).

West India Dock Tavern   A large tavern built on the corner of Cold Harbour and later-named Preston's Rd. in 1830. Not a success, it was demolished in the 1850s. The present-day houses 37 to 45 Cold Harbour are more or less on the site of the tavern.

West India Docks   The West India Docks were constructed in two phases. The two northern-most docks were constructed between 1800 and 1802. The southern-most dock, the South West India Dock, later known as South Dock, was constructed in the 1860s, replacing the City Canal. The docks closed in 1980, and the area has since been subject to significant office development centred on Canary Wharf.

West India Docks Impounding Station   Built in 1928 and located at what was once the western entrance to the City Canal, the still-operational impounding station pumps river water into the West India Docks, to maintain the docks' water level.

55. Impounding station, left of the City Pride (Arms)

Westwood, Baillie & Co Robert Baillie and Joseph Westwood started their career working for Ditchburn & Mare in Orchard Place. In 1857, along with James Campbell, they opened their own shipbuilding yard at London Yard, off Manchester Rd. With the decline of Thames shipbuilding in the 1870s, the company changed direction to specialise in iron and steel engineering (bridge building in particular). The firm was wound up in 1893, but Westwood continued at his own engineering site at Napier Yard and (later) on Harbinger Rd.

Wharf Rd. The eastern part of this road was renamed Saunders Ness Rd. in 1937. The western part was renamed Ferry St. a year later.

Windmill Tavern Beer house at the end of Claude St., close to Millwall Pier, part of a jumble of wooden structures built around the windmill (which was built in 1701). The windmill and all the buildings burned down in January 1884.

Yarrow House Block of flats on Glengall Rd. (later Tiller Rd.) which was destroyed during WWII. Named after Sir Alfred Yarrow.

Yarrow's (1842-1932) Engineering and shipbuilding company that started business at Folly Wall in 1865, concentrating later on military vessels. The company moved to London Yard in 1898.

Z Warehouse One of the first Millwall Docks warehouses, built in 1870 on the Millwall Outer Dock. It was partially demolished in 1933 to make room for an extension of McDougall's Wheatsheaf Mill.

Photo Credits

Kathy Hawkins: 41, 51

Peter Wright: 1, 2, 3, 5, 12, 14, 43, 45, 50, 55

Mick Lemmerman: 4, 26, 28, 36, 39, 44

Island History Trust Collection: 6, 7, 8, 10, 17, 27, 31, 35, 37, 52

Christine Coleman: 11

Kathy Duggan: 13, 32

Gary Wood: 19

Tony Clary: 20

Emma Tarbard: 21, 23

Jackie Jordan Wade: 24

Arthur Ayres: 29

John Salmon: 30

Martin Tucker: 53

Printed in Great Britain
by Amazon.co.uk, Ltd.,
Marston Gate.